W9-AUT-137

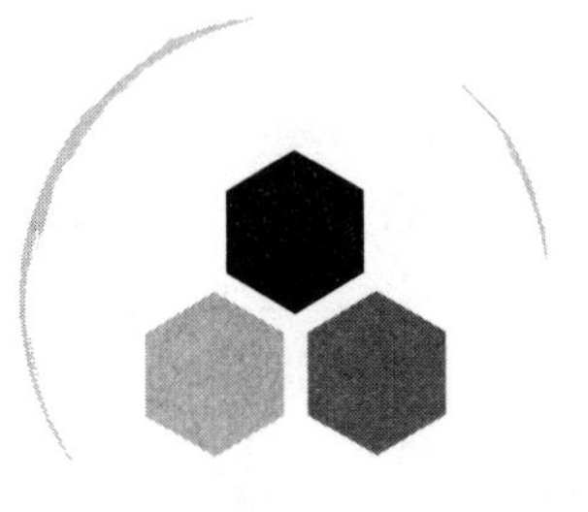

beyond soccer

The ultimate goal

by Rich Daughtridge

Beyond Soccer

McDougal Publishing is a ministry of the The McDougal Foundation, Inc., a Maryland nonprofit corporation dedicated to spreading the Gospel of the Lord Jesus Christ to as many people as possible in the shortest time possible.

Published by:

McDougal Publishing
P.O. Box 3595
Hagerstown, MD 21742-3595

www.mcdougalpublishing.com

ISBN 1-58158-065-7 Trade Paper
ISBN 1-58158-070-3 Hardback

Printed in the United States of America
For Worldwide Distribution

Dedication

This book is dedicated to you: the players, coaches, and fans.

My prayer is that this book will become a companion to you in your daily walk with God and that it will offer you a resource for your Christian growth.

Acknowledgments

Special thanks to:

My wife, Susan, for all your love and patience during this journey.

My son, Reed, for being a daily reminder to me of what life is all about.

My Mom and Dad, for all your sacrifice and love.

My family in Maryland and North Carolina, for all your support over the years.

My coaches and teammates along the way, for your insight and friendship.

Contents

From the Author

My drive from Baltimore that day seemed longer than usual as thoughts that my playing days were over raced through my mind. I had struggled for two years to become a regular on the roster, and now after three weeks into pre-season this year, my chances of being signed to a contract were fading. I had a wonderful wife and a bouncing baby boy waiting at home. I loved my job as a web designer, and chances are my dog, Jake, would be on the back porch eager to see me after a hard day's work. But the knot in my stomach was telling me that soccer might be over. I pulled off the exit, stared at my cell phone, and dialed the coach's number… "Coach. I've decided to step away."

It was one of those moments when I realized I needed to readjust my priorities and begin living life beyond soccer. I was holding on too tightly to a boyhood dream. It was time to put God first again and let Him lead.

I grew up in Hagerstown, Maryland, knowing only one thing—soccer. I began playing in youth soccer leagues at the age of five and moved on to the club level for the Hagerstown Soccer Club and eventually Potomac Silver Streak, just outside Washington, D.C. In the small town of Smithsburg, Maryland, known for its annual Steam and Craft Show, the Dixie Eatery restaurant and football, I somehow made a name for myself at Smithsburg High as the football place kicker and "the guy who's good at soccer." I would meet my future wife, Susan, on the sidelines of those playing fields. A cheerleader then, she always offered encouragement and the advice I didn't always want, but needed to hear. As high school began to come to an end, the college search was on and I traveled on recruiting visits to different colleges on the East Coast. As I compared the soccer programs, academics, cafeteria food and living conditions of them all, I ended up choosing the odd one out of the bunch, Virginia Military Institute.

VMI refined some of the attributes of my personality as the challenges brought forth from a military environment helped me excel in the classroom and on the soccer field. Visits from Susan and my family on the weekends kept me sane and I graduated with a great education and a record-breaking soccer career I was proud of. I was then off to try to carve out a niche for myself in the world of professional soccer.

During a two-year period, I played for the Hampton Roads Mariners and the Charlotte Eagles during the summers, while coaching soccer as the assistant coach at Washington and Lee University during the rest of the year. Great experiences and lots of fun, but the paychecks made me realize that playing and coaching soccer would not be a long-term career option. With a laptop, a how-to web design book, and a cardboard box for a desk, I started a small web design business.

The time came when Susan and I, now married, decided to forgo more traveling and uncertainty and move back to the Hagerstown/ Smithsburg area to settle down. The web design business was growing steadily, the soccer camp I started the previous summer was now up to four weeks of sessions, and Susan was able to use her college degree in a job she enjoyed. Recreational indoor and outdoor soccer leagues were my outlets for playing the game until a friend said he knew the coach of the Baltimore Blast and would call to set up a tryout before the upcoming season.

My experience with the Blast was exciting, and it was fun to play at the professional level again. It was clear that God had granted me a "desire of my heart" again. Ups and downs would characterize the next two and a half years with the Blast as I went through the excitement of playing each weekend and then the despair of sitting on the bench for extended periods. As I began the juggling act between soccer, traveling the road, business and family, it became clear that soccer was fading. My choice to either become a regular player on the team or step away was clear.

I believe that much of life is about readjusting our priorities and trusting God to help us in our journey. So many times our selfishness and human nature pull us towards doing the things we want to do, while learning to ignore the whisper of what we should do. In my case soccer is a priority that gets in the way. In your case it may be your job, your friends or just wanting to have fun.

As I pulled back onto the highway that afternoon, the vacuum that I thought I'd feel was replaced with a sense of peace. I knew at that moment that God was in control.

The next three months I watched my new baby grow and appreciated every minute. On the weekends I still glanced at my watch in the evenings wondering what the score might be at the Blast game that night. One afternoon in December, I sat working in the office when my cell phone went off behind me. The voice on the other end was the new coach for the Blast, hired just before Christmas, halfway through the season…"We are interested in having you give it another go. Can you come down for practice in the morning?"

At the time I write this book, I recently celebrated winning the national championship with the Blast in Milwaukee. I've learned that life is about letting go and letting God.

I don't know what my future is as a professional soccer player, but I do know who holds the future.

Perspective

Philippians 4:11-12 *I am not saying this because I am in need, for I have learned to be content whatever the circumstances. I know what it is to be in need, and I know what it is to have plenty. I have learned the secret of being content in any and every situation, whether well fed or hungry, whether living in plenty or in want.*

Someone once said the true definition of contentment is being thankful for what you already have. That truth was revealed to me when I had an opportunity to travel to Africa and see firsthand how different cultures live. I was walking through a crowded downtown market in Morocco, shopping for souvenirs, when I was distracted by loud, sharp noises and laughing children. As the scene came into focus, I saw there were young children kicking and chasing an old can through the courtyard, using it as a soccer ball. I stopped to watch for a minute, astonished by the joy on their faces, and compared the hard, dirty concrete under their battered shoes to the lush, green fields I was accustomed to in our country. These kids knew nothing else. They only knew they loved to play soccer.

We should be thankful for what we have and take the focus off of what we want.

It's times like this you realize why we should be thankful for what we have and take the focus off of what we want. It reminds us perhaps how much we complain about the little things: that person driving too slow in front of us, how we wish we made more money or the simple irritation from waiting in the checkout line too long.

When Paul wrote, *"I have learned to be content whatever the circumstances,"* he was speaking from experience. He wrote these words while sitting in a dreary prison cell, yet his tone is full of tenderness, warmth and joy. We will all face times when we feel trapped in the middle of adverse circumstances, but how we react is all in our perspective.

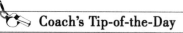

Coach's Tip-of-the-Day

Sprints are a normal and healthy part of soccer practices to help build the fitness level of your team when needed. Sometimes, however, it is just as effective to encourage a high-intensity small-sided game and as a reward, give the team the day off. This will instill within the players a desire to practice hard and raise their focus level.

Player's Tip-of-the-Day

Tryouts can be an intimidating experience for any level soccer player from youth to professional. One way to quickly gather some confidence in these situations is to begin talking and communicating on the field immediately. Instructing other players and asking for the ball yourself will set the tone for your game that day, giving you the needed confidence to make an impact.

Shocking the World

Philippians 4:13 *I can do everything through him who gives me strength.*

During the 1950 FIFA World Cup in Brazil, the United States national team, made up of part-timers and a few ex-professionals from overseas, took the field against England, a team unbeaten since World War Two. With all the fanfare and history that surrounded English soccer, the United States was sure to be a small stepping stone in England's quest for the coveted World Cup trophy. The score remained tied throughout most of the first half, but Haitian-American Joe Gaetjens scored a dramatic header just before the halftime whistle to give the Yanks a 1-0 lead. The English side came out strong the second half, creating many opportunities, but the Americans held on to their lead and sent the English squad away in disbelief. It was a story of David and Goliath, an upset that shocked the entire soccer world.

It was a story of David and Goliath, an upset that shocked the entire soccer world.

Sometimes we face schedules, deadlines and what seem to be unaccomplishable goals, but God reminds us that we can do *"everything through him."*

In this passage, we see that God doesn't expect us to rely on our own understanding or abilities, but rather to seek Him for the physical and mental strength we'll need to succeed.

Coach's Tip-of-the-Day

"World Cup" is a fun game that can be played with players of all ages. Everyone is split up into groups of two and told to choose a country as their team name. Cones are placed about 5 yards out from the goal where no player can enter, but must shoot from behind these cones. All the balls are placed in the goal as the coach or one volunteer acts as the goalie, throwing one or more balls that everyone scrambles to get control of and score. Once a team scores, they celebrate by yelling their country name and jogging off behind the goal to wait for the next round. The last team left is eliminated from the game. The rest of the players return for additional rounds. The final round, when only two countries remain, will decide the "World-Cup" champion.
See a diagram of this drill at beyondsoccer.org.

Player's Tip-of-the-Day

When practicing shooting, try to create game-like situations. Instead of shooting a ball sitting still, have the goalkeeper kick or throw the ball out with some pace. Concentrate on taking a nice, controlling touch, then strike the ball. By practicing shooting in this way, you will better prepare yourself for the shooting opportunities that come in a game.

Who You Are When No One Is Looking

by Kelly Findley, College Soccer Coach

Colossians 4:17 *Tell Archippus: "See to it that you complete the work you have received in the Lord."*
Colossians 3:23-24 *Whatever you do, work at it with all your heart, as working for the Lord, not for men, since you know that you will receive an inheritance from the Lord as a reward. It is the Lord Christ you are serving.*
Ephesians 6:5-6 *Slaves, obey your earthly masters with respect and fear, and with sincerity of heart, just as you would obey Christ. Obey them not only to win their favor when their eye is on you, but like slaves of Christ, doing the will of God from your heart.*

As an athlete you are constantly confronted with choices that can range from how to react to a belligerent opponent to running every sprint as hard as you can or loafing when the coach isn't looking. Your demeanor in these situations can be, depending on how you react, a testimony and an opportunity to worship the Lord.

Whatever you do, whether in word or deed, do it all in the name of the Lord Jesus.

Every team must be fit to be successful, and that means sprints, agility, plyometrics and the list goes on. Every sprint you make as an athlete has a choice: do I touch the line or do I almost touch the line. Who are you when no one but the Lord is looking? Colossians 3:23-24 says: "*Whatever you do, work at it with all your heart, as working for the Lord, not for men!*" You are not here to impress men or coaches with your work and the Lord sees everything you do. So if you want your effort in soccer to glorify God, you must work at it with all your heart as working for the Lord and not working to please your coach but to please our Father.

It might be a little thing to worry about, like touching the line during sprints, but if you can win the little battles every day through serving the Lord *"and whatever you do, whether in word or deed, do it all in the name of the Lord Jesus, giving thanks to God the Father through him"* Colossians 3:17, you will win the big battles when you come up against them.

Coach's Tip-of-the-Day

Demand character from your players and remind them that what they do when no one is looking matters more than they know. The off-season is the best time for players to put these words into action because there is no one watching most of the time and they must motivate themselves to do the workouts. But if they are working for the Lord, they will look at that workout from a completely different perspective.

Player's Tip-of-the-Day

One thing I always disliked as a player was when we were doing sprints and the coach told us ahead of time that we were going to do ten and I would work as hard as I could for everyone as a teammate of mine took it easy for three and pushed for one. Then the coach would call out that whoever wins the next sprint was done with fitness, and sure enough my teammate who had been coasting would win and be done with fitness. That used to make me crazy!!! Fitness is necessary and you never want to loaf but when you are working for the Lord (Colossians 3:17) you'd better give Him everything you have because He deserves it!!! Honor Him with your effort in everything you do.

For more information about today's guest writer, Kelly Findley, log on to beyondsoccer.org.

The Brazilian Warm-up

Psalm 25: 4-5 *Show me your ways, O Lord , teach me your paths; guide me in your truth and teach me, for you are God my Savior, and my hope is in you all day long.*

As a youth player some years ago, the team I was on had a pregame warm-up known as "The Brazilian." It consisted of lining up on one sideline and jogging in unison side by side across the field. The captain would yell out different variations such as knees up, heels up, etc., and at once the team would adjust to all doing the same thing. As we neared the end of the warm-up, we would increase our speed to 50%, 75% and then a few 100% sprints so our muscles were ready to go for the game ahead. A period of stretching then followed. The tournaments were always the toughest as you tried to work out the soreness from the game that morning and get ready to play yet another game.

In our busy lifestyles, one of the hardest things to do in our Christian walk is taking the time each day to spend with God, the daily time to warm-up our minds and stretch our thinking. Our world throws so many things at us that contradict and undermine our beliefs that we need to continually be refueled by God.

Our world throws so many things at us that contradict and undermine our beliefs that we need to continually be refueled by God.

It's always obvious to me when I go through a period when I don't take a quiet time in the mornings. My personality becomes short-tempered and my thoughts begin to wander. The moment I get back on track, my attitude comes back into focus.

Because so many people are affected by our actions and words each day, it makes it so important to be focused on God for the sake of these people. We are evangelizing and representing God without even directly talking about Him. People see that there is "something different" about us. This difference can only come when we are tuned in to God and His Holy Spirit. Make it a point to schedule an appointment with God each day.

Coach's Tip-of-the-Day

Try this warm-up sometime with your team, while you participate as the leader giving instructions. Some ideas for variations: knees up, heels up (or kick-your-butt), skip, skip and cross your arms in front, down-with-the-right hand (touching your right hand to the ground), down-with-the-left hand, jump for a header, side-to-side, backwards, karaoke, 50% sprint, 75% sprint and 100% sprint. Sometimes becoming involved in your team's warm-up in this way can help develop a bond between you and your players.

Player's Tip-of-the-Day

It's always important to take a good warm-up before a practice or game. Once warmed up try to take some time to do things you'll be doing in a game. If you are a defender, drive some long balls to a teammate. As a goalie, you will certainly want to make some saves. Those taking most of the shots in a game, forwards and midfielders, should take this opportunity to strike some balls at the goalkeeper.

The World His Stage

by Steve Teel, Very Bold Ministries

1 Timothy 4:12 *Don't let anyone look down on you because you are young, but set an example for the believers in speech, in life, in love, in faith and in purity.*

One of the great individual World Cup soccer performances of all time came in 1958. The player who led Brazil to the championship against Sweden was Pele.

The first two games of the tournament, Brazil played without Pele, who was injured. In the third match, Pele played and Brazil beat Russia and advanced to the next round. The forward failed to score, but his great talent was apparent. In the quarterfinals, he scored his first goal, leading his country to a 1-0 win over Wales. In the semifinals, Pele scored three second-half goals in a 5-2 win over France.

God often chooses unlikely candidates to display His greatness.

In the championship, Brazil would face the host country, Sweden, in Stockholm. The game would turn with Pele's magic. With Brazil leading the Swedes 2-1, Pele unleashed what is known as one of the greatest goals ever. As sportswriter Simon Gonzalez describes it, [Pele] "had his back to the net and a defender closely marking him. His teammate passed to him anyway, a looping ball he received with his thigh. He neatly trapped it, then let the ball drop to his foot and flicked it back over his head. He spun around the startled defender, and volleyed a shot into the back of the net past a diving goalie."

The greatest player on the greatest team also added the final goal of the World Cup on a header to give his country a 5-2 win. Pele had scored two goals in the World Cup final and had scored an amazing six goals in Brazil's last three games.

Now listen to this. Pele was not a veteran accustomed to the world as his stage. No, the best player of the World Cup was only 17 years old when he led Brazil to victory. Still just a teenager, Pele established himself as the ultimate soccer player of the world.

The world had seen not only that a young person could play soccer with older, more experienced men, but also that a teenager could dominate the game. The world does not often give young people such opportunities. But God does give opportunities to young people.

God often chooses unlikely candidates to display His greatness. When Jesus selected His disciples, He did not choose the most likely or obvious group of people. Instead of religious leaders, Jesus chose fishermen and other normal people. They were ordinary, unschooled people. Yet Jesus entrusted them to carry His message to the world. Jesus was thankful for God's plan to use this group of people, saying, "*I praise you, Father, Lord of heaven and earth, because you have hidden these things from the wise and learned, and revealed them to little children. Yes, Father, for this was your good pleasure.*" Matthew 11:25-26

It is God's good pleasure to use unlikely candidates. It is God's joy and delight to use children and youth to carry His message. It is God's pleasure to use you. Ask God to use you. He will give you the opportunities to witness to the world of His great love.

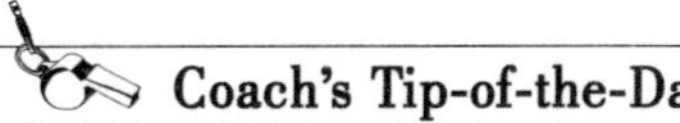

Coach's Tip-of-the-Day

Circuit training is a practice drill that can be used both as a warm-up and as a fitness exercise. Around the field, different stations are set up to indicate particular exercises. One station may be toe taps on the ball, foundations (knocking the ball between your feet), push-ups, sit-ups, shuttle runs, agility training, dribbling through cones, pressure training, juggling or any other individual or partner drill that can be done in a small space. The team is split up into groups of two. At the starting point the first group goes with each group following after the first group finishes the first exercise. The circuit can be repeated two or more times depending on the intensity and age level.
See a diagram of this drill at beyondsoccer.org.

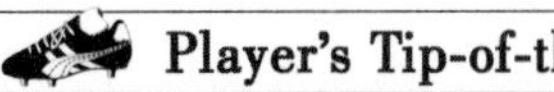

Player's Tip-of-the-Day

Agility training is an important part of effective soccer conditioning. Here are two simple agility drills:
1) Line Hops – Starting with both feet to the side of a line, hop from side to side as fast as possible for intervals of 30 seconds. Switch to hopping on the right foot only for 30 seconds. Start on the opposite side and hop with the left foot only for 30 seconds. Continue alternating for two or more sets.
2) Cone Hops w/ Ball – Have a partner kneel with a ball in his or her hands a few feet away facing the person working. As the player hops over the cone, the partner rolls the ball on the ground for the player to pass back. Work for about 30 seconds and then switch partners.
See a diagram of this drill at beyondsoccer.org.

For more information about today's guest writer, Steve Teel, log on to beyondsoccer.org.

The Off-season

Lamentations 3:25 (NASB) *The Lord is good to those who wait for Him, to the person who seeks Him.*

Soccer is one of the most difficult sports to train for in the off-season. It has often been said the only way to prepare for a soccer season is to play as much as you can. The mixture of endurance conditioning and speed training makes soccer unique among sports such as basketball, football and baseball. A soccer player must have the ability to run for 90 minutes, while changing speed and direction constantly throughout the game. To try to get ready for a season by going out and jogging 3 miles at a comfortable pace a few times a week doesn't cut it. Only the right mixture of long-distance running, weight lifting, sprint workouts, plyometrics and actual playing can best prepare a player.

In the game of life, we also have our in-seasons and off-seasons. There are those times in the thick of the battle when our jobs are stressful as we sprint to meet quarterly quotas and deadlines, our schedule seems too busy to keep up, or we cram to prepare for the three big tests that just happen to fall on the same Friday. As we seek to find answers, peace and a sense of hope during these times, doesn't our prayer life improve? We tend to become closer to God in these circumstances. The opposite is true when things are going well. We just received the promotion, profits went up, the test scores came back positive and we feel like all things around us are coming together. During these times, we often become complacent and become comfort-

In the game of life, we also have our in-seasons and off-seasons.

able as Christians. God becomes an after-thought. It's important to develop a consistent prayer life, learn about His Word, and prepare for the in-seasons of life, because when those times come, when the whistle blows and it's time to start the game, we're ready spiritually to handle it and react in a way that pleases God.

Coach's Tip-of-the-Day

In the off-season, reflect on the previous season and take time to research new drills and coaching techniques. The Internet is a great place to start. If possible, attend a state coaching convention or even the National Soccer Coaching Association of America annual convention to learn from the leaders in the sport. These conventions cover everything from nutrition to real-life coaching scenarios.

Player's Tip-of-the-Day

An effective off-season workout consists of combining sprinting drills with endurance training. A simple track workout can be sprinting the straightaways and jogging the turns. A distance of 2-4 miles is normally a good goal. Four laps around a standard size track is 1 mile. To develop the touch on the ball, you may consider juggling during the breaks, perhaps between each mile.

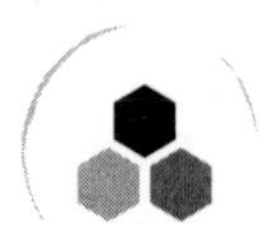

One Winner

by Rusty Bryant, Brilla Soccer Ministries

1 Corinthians 9:24-25 *Do you not know that in a race all the runners run, but only one gets the prize? Run in such a way as to get the prize. Everyone who competes in the games goes into strict training. They do it to get a crown that will not last; but we do it to get a crown that will last forever.*

Have you ever competed in any athletic event where more than one person or more than one team could emerge as the winner? I can't think of any right now. In fact, every competition can have only *one* winner. Even when a tie is permitted, it is never considered two "winners."

Run in such a way as to get the prize.

I have seen several instances in which there were "almost" *two* winners, but each time, only *one* winner emerged. When I was ten years old, I had a "scratch-off" card from a local grocery store that gave me a shot at winning $500 in a horse race. I watched the horse race on TV that night, and I cheered as hard as I could for horse #3. As the race came to an end, my horse was dead even with another horse. As they crossed the finish line, it looked as though they had crossed simultaneously. As a ten-year-old boy, I knew that I had won. By the looks of things on the TV, my horse had at least *tied* the other horse. Surely that was good for some of that $500. However, the slow motion replay showed that the other horse had won by the length of a "horse's nose." That's right, I was *that* close to winning. But there was only one winner that day, and it wasn't me. What did I get for coming in a close second? Nothing!

"Do you not know that in a race all the runners run, but only one

gets the prize? Run in such a way as to get the prize." 1 Corinthians 9:24

Only one winner emerges in an athletic event. Play in such a way that you will win the prize!

Wait a second, though! Don't overlook the rest of what Paul has to say:

"Everyone who competes in the games goes into strict training. They do it to get a crown that will not last: but we do it to get a crown that will last forever." 1 Corinthians 9:25

As you compete to win in sports, don't forget that the prizes associated with living the Christian life will last forever! The crowns that last forever are not here on earth, but are awaiting us in Heaven!

Coach's Tip-of-the-Day

Praise in public, correct in private. When possible, a rule of thumb in coaching is to encourage players when they are doing well in a tone that others can hear, but if correction is needed, don't make a public proclamation about it, but rather pull the players aside or correct them at a closer distance. This will especially help younger players avoid embarrassment and create an environment of respect at practice.

Player's Tip-of-the-Day

Pressure training on the ground: This is a great drill for two players to work on their touch and cardio. Place two cones about 10 feet apart. One player kneels in the middle about 10 feet back, making a triangle with the cones. The kneeling player rolls a ball on the ground to the outside of the cone, while the other player runs to meet the ball and passes with his or her outside foot back to the other player. The runner then hurries to the other side to receive another ball. Take turns doing 45-second intervals. The next variation consists of placing the two cones side by side. The runner in this case hops over the cones and passes the ball back as fast as possible.
See a diagram of this drill at beyondsoccer.org.

For more information about today's guest writer, Rusty Bryant, log on to beyondsoccer.org.

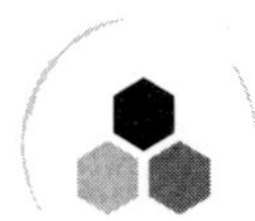

The Hand of God

Deuteronomy 5:15 (NASB) *" 'You shall remember that you were a slave in the land of Egypt, and the LORD your God brought you out of there by a mighty hand and by an outstretched arm; therefore the LORD your God commanded you to observe the sabbath day.' "*

In the 1986 World Cup, Diego Maradona of Argentina electrified the world with his talent, quickness and goal scoring ability. As a teenager, he scored more goals than anyone else and ultimately led Argentina to a World Cup championship. In the third game of the tournament, Argentina faced England, another soccer-rich country expected to do well that year. As a cross came in from the left side in the 50th minute, Maradona jumped to meet the ball just past the outstretched arms of Peter Shilton, England's world-renowned goalkeeper. In a split second Maradona, realizing the ball was out of reach, quickly raised his right arm and redirected the ball with his fist into the net. The referees, shielded from the play, all missed it and the goal stood as the Argentine players smothered Maradona in celebration. Photographs would later confirm the hand ball and the goal became known as "the hand of God."

> *You will one day look back in amazement at how the hand of God led you to where you are today.*

Although this sports highlight is not biblical in nature, we can certainly find parallels in our Christian walk. How many times have we tried to go it on our own? Or maybe some of you may have always relied on your self, and never felt the need to rely on God. When we seek God, our lives are blessed. In the study guide

Experiencing God: Knowing and Doing the Will of God by Henry Blackaby and Claude King, the authors outline four places to look for God's will and perfect plan for our lives: the Bible, prayer, circumstances and the Church. These four, when considered together, help us understand God's will for our lives. As you begin to follow Him and make Him a part of every decision in your life, you will one day look back in amazement at how the hand of God led you to where you are today.

Coach's Tip-of-the-Day

Heading is an important skill to learn in today's game. For youth players, try teaching the fundamentals of contacting the ball on the forehead by having players work with a partner at close range. Start by having one of the players sit while the other tosses the ball for his or her partner to head back. Switch after about a minute or so and then progress to kneeling, standing and, finally, jumping. Proper technique and practice can help avoid injuries and allow younger players a chance to become comfortable heading a soccer ball.

Player's Tip-of-the-Day

Pattern juggling is a good way to develop skills and break the monotony when training alone. Taking two touches on your right foot and then two touches on your left foot and back again is just one example. This ability to command the ball can greatly enhance your touch and feel for the ball. Furthermore, this forces you to take more touches with your weaker foot than you might if juggling simply to keep the ball in the air.

David Ran

1 Samuel 17:48 *As the Philistine moved closer to attack him,* ***David ran quickly*** *toward the battle line to meet him.*

You may have heard the story of David and Goliath before, but when you read the passage above, did you stop to think about how David reacted in this situation? He ran! Picture the scene. David and the army of the Israelites stand on a hill trying to figure out how to defeat the Philistines on the opposite hill. Not to mention there's an 8-foot-tall Philistine named Goliath intimidating everyone with verbal threats. Doesn't Goliath seem like one of those guys in high school who is the typical bully? He seems like an All-State wrestler and football linebacker, blessed with muscle and size, who thrives on stuffing the school chess club members in their locker. David on the other hand seems like the typical soccer player. He wasn't blessed with a ton of pure strength, was not extremely tall, but probably was quicker than most other guys his age. Against the odds, David reacts to Goliath with utter confidence, courage and faith. David didn't even wear armor, but rather took only "five smooth stones" to the fight, adding to his list of disadvantages. But he ran. He ran knowing that God would take care of him in the midst of the storm. How often do we rely on God with that much faith? To trust Him in our finances, our job, our schoolwork, during the game or in the midst of tragedy. David is an example of how we all should live, running to God with our desires and our hurts, trusting that His perfect will be done in our lives each day.

David ran quickly toward the battle line.

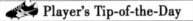

Coach's Tip-of-the-Day

When coaching youth players it is always a good idea to mix drills with fun games that emphasize the skills for that day. Furthermore, letting the team know that there will be a game next if they "work hard for the next 15 minutes" will increase their concentration and focus on the activity.

Player's Tip-of-the-Day

Weight lifting can be a valuable aspect of a soccer player's training when done correctly. Keep a good balance between heavy weights at low repetitions and lighter weights using high repetitions. Most soccer players should work to develop strength, but focus on doing 8 to 12 reps of the exercise most of the time. This method will develop strength while maintaining the agility needed on the soccer field. Doing low reps (2 to 4) while using heavy weights could cause a player to "bulk up" too much. Weight training can also be used as a confidence builder. Some players even make it a point to get a light jog, lift and stretch the morning of a game.

Chameleon Christians

by Joe Bean, College Soccer Coach

Philippians 1:27 *Whatever happens, conduct yourselves in a manner worthy of the gospel of Christ. Then, whether I come and see you or only hear about you in my absence, I will know that you stand firm in one spirit, contending as one man for the faith of the gospel.*

Several years ago my granddaughter was excited to show me her new "pet," a chameleon. As you know, a chameleon changes its color to blend in with the surrounding terrain and is easily lost to anyone who owns it. It wasn't very long before little Brittnie had no pet. Mr. Chameleon had gone his own merry way without anyone knowing the difference. We as Christians need to be aware of the way in which we conduct ourselves or we can easily fall into the "chameleon camouflage" of our Christianity. We need to be visible to all we come in contact with and not hide our convictions and beliefs behind secular standards or mores. The verse refers to "whatever happens" so that our conduct stays aboveboard, with integrity and with Christ-like actions.

We need to be visible to all we come in contact and not hide our convictions and beliefs behind secular standards or mores.

What a challenge to a soccer team that is under pressure to withstand poor officiating, dirty tactics from an opponent or the temptation to lash out verbally against teammates, officials or opposing players.

Our objective should be, as Christians, to be both vulnerable and transparent in all we do, not getting "lost" in the world like a chameleon.

Coach's Tip-of-the-Day

One of the best drills to help develop touch and confidence with the ball is to have all your players within a given area, e.g., the center circle, each with his or her own ball. Upon your signal they begin dribbling in and out of each other, forcing them to look up, work around an opponent and work in their change of pace and feinting. It should be done in intervals of two to three minutes. The "rest" period for two minutes would be to juggle the ball until the next round. Fifteen minutes of this will also help to develop fitness.

Player's Tip-of-the-Day

As a player who wants to be the best that you can be, you should spend as much time with the soccer ball as possible. It has been said that the best coach a player can have is his or her soccer ball. Using the ball to dribble, feint, juggle or pound against a wall and "catch" it are all ways to build up your touch as well as your confidence. Some of the best players I have had over the years I would find in the gym at all hours of the day and night working with the ball. It will pay off!!

For more information about today's guest writer, Joe Bean, log on to beyondsoccer.org.

Communication

Psalm 5:3 *In the morning, O LORD, you hear my voice; in the morning I lay my requests before you and* ***wait*** *in expectation.*

One of the most important characteristics of a successful soccer team is the players' ability to communicate on the field. "Man on!" "Turn!" "Square!" When players on a team have developed the skill of instructing each other on and off the ball, the team keeps possession more, makes better decisions as a unit and generates confidence within the group. I had a coach who always said that communication is two-way. It involves talking to your teammates as well as listening to instructions. A teammate can yell "Man on," but the player with the ball must decide after hearing the instruction to play the ball back or take the ball out of the pressure situation to keep possession. If that same player decides to go with his or her instincts and play a dangerous ball, the chances of the team losing the ball or creating a counterattack for the opponents increase. This would be described as a breakdown in communication. Many times I find myself waking up in the morning, reading my devotional, going through a bulleted-list prayer in my mind and then it's on to my Eggo waffles and the second cup of coffee. I rarely take the time to listen to what God may want to say to me, to meditate on the things I've just prayed about and ask God for direction and peace of mind for the day ahead. It's amazing what things come to the forefront of your mind when you are still and waiting, things that the noise of

In our fast paced society, don't forget to listen and be still in God's presence.

the world seems to drown out, things that when you stop to think about them totally make sense and offer a sense of understanding. In our fast-paced society, don't forget to listen and be still in God's presence. The communication that results could mean the difference between winning and losing.

Coach's Tip-of-the-Day

Sequence passing is a great drill for players of all ages to learn communication and possession skills. Break the team up into three or four even groups with different colored pennies and have each player in the groups count off from 1 to 7 (or however many are on each team). Explain to the team now… No. 1 will pass to No. 2, who would pass to No. 3, then to No. 4, until No. 7 receives the ball and passes the ball back to No. 1. Then it starts all over again. With the three teams spread out in approximately a 60 x 80 yard grid, players are forced to keep their heads up and find their teammates who are also instructed to jog continually throughout the grid away from their teammates until it's time to receive the ball. Do not allow the groups to huddle in one area. In the first phase of the drill, instruct them that they cannot talk at all, but rather keep their heads up to constantly find their teammates. After some time of silence, instruct the team to pick up the pace by sprinting to receive the ball now and allow the the players to talk. You should see a gradual increase in the quality of play. Reward them for their efforts and explain the importance of communication on the field.
See a diagram of this drill at beyondsoccer.org.

Player's Tip-of-the-Day

All soccer players must possess the ability to communicate on the field. If your personality is on the quiet side, force yourself and make it a point to talk more on the field. If you're not bashful, make sure your instructions are positive and constructive.

Wounded

Hebrews 10: 24-25 *And let us consider how we may spur one another on toward love and good deeds. Let us not give up meeting together, as some are in the habit of doing, but let us encourage one another—and all the more as you see the Day approaching.*

It could be argued that soccer is not the most dangerous sport when compared to the brutality of football or hockey. On the other hand, considering the fact that only shin guards are worn for protection, we could make a case that soccer is dangerous in it's own right. It's probably true that soccer is not subject to as many concussions or serious injuries compared to some other sports, but soccer players may suffer from more nagging injuries such as ankle sprains, pulled muscles, deep muscle bruises and others. These injuries, although painful, can be played through without many people knowing it. A sprained ankle is oftentimes taped up, or a hamstring strain is wrapped with a compression sleeve. The player feels the nagging pain, but others probably don't notice.

Doesn't it feel like God slaps you upside the head sometimes?

I said all this to help draw an analogy between these hidden physical pains and the emotional pain that so many of the people around us feel.

I was getting ready to start a workout at the gym the other day, when an acquaintance stopped to talk. After about a minute or so of small talk, I was thinking to myself, "I need to get going with this workout so I can go back to the office!" The small talk continued into a conversation, as I finished up my ab workout (which I had been doing while talking?!). After about five minutes or so and my annoyance growing, this person began to tell me the reason he had changed jobs a few months ago. Talking further, he told me his father was sick and may not make it much longer.

Doesn't it feel like God slaps you upside the head sometimes? Here I am with my ever-so-important, retentive-time-efficient agenda that I can't sense a person who is hurting and just needed someone to talk to. We get so busy and self-centered that we forget the wounds that so many people have around us: the pain from losing a loved one, the struggles in their family, or just the longing for a lasting sense of hope in a world that dishes out temporary fixes. Pray for the ability to daily keep the Holy Spirit leading and guiding you in your relationships with others, that your eyes may be open to the hurt around you.

Coach's Tip-of-the-Day

Most athletic trainers would agree that the best way to take care of nagging injuries is to heat before and ice after. In other words, warming up a muscle or muscles by using a heat pack, a whirlpool, or a longer warm-up can help. Once the practice or game is finished, cooling down with an ice pack for fifteen minutes can help reduce swelling and irritation. Furthermore, it is helpful between activities, perhaps in the evenings, to alternate sessions of heat and ice, to further aid the rehabilitation.

Player's Tip-of-the-Day

When injured for more than a couple of days, it's important to continue working out in some fashion to maintain your fitness level. Your body is conditioned and you've worked hard to develop endurance and strength. Riding a bike can oftentimes be an alternative to running and reduces impact on specific muscles while still offering a cardiovascular workout.

Peace, Love and Soccer

by John Spracklin, Professional Soccer Chaplain

Ephesians 4:3 *Make every effort to keep the unity of the Spirit through the bond of peace.*

Colombia is a country united by soccer but badly divided by civil war. For the past twenty years the government has been in a bloody battle with powerful drug lords and communist guerillas. Bombs, kidnappings and countless murders have virtually destroyed this beautiful country.

Seeking to be known for its soccer, not its violence, Colombia petitioned for the 2001 Copa America, a tournament for all the national teams of South America. Pastrana, head of the Copa America tournament committee, said, "The country wants not only to hold the Copa America but also to demonstrate ... before the world that what we want is peace and reconciliation between Colombians." The Colombian government promised sufficient security and said it had made a pact with the drug traffickers not to disrupt the tournament. Colombia's president lobbied hard for the event, and rebel officials said that its members were soccer fans and that they would not disturb the tournament.

When we put down our differences and focus on what we share, we find joy and peace ...

At first rebels struggled to carry through with their promise as a month later the tournament was put on hold when one of the tournament officials was kidnapped. But at the urging of the Colombian people, the captors released the official and the tournament was called to resume.

When it came time to play, Colombia was ready. They rolled

through the first stage of the tournament by beating Venezuela 2-0, Ecuador 1-0 and Chile 2-0. They breezed by Peru in the quarterfinals 3-0 and topped Honduras 2-0 to reach the finals. The nation was in a jubilant mood. Fans packed the streets waving Colombian flags. Following the win, the national newspaper's headline read, "A Cup Full of Joy." Touched by the nation's ability to lay down its violence and support its team, tournament leaders began calling it "The Peace Cup."

Inspired by fans, the Colombian team — a team that was not supposed to make the finals — exceeded all expectations by winning the tournament with a 1-0 win. As the final whistle blew, the crowd waved Colombian flags and chanted, "We want peace." For the first time in years Colombia was once again united. They rejoiced together instead of fighting over their differences.

As children of God we need to remember that we share God's Spirit, the greatest treasure of all. The Holy Spirit unites all God's children into a peaceful relationship with each other. Since we share so many things in common, our disagreements should not prevent us from enjoying these together. And as this story illustrates… when we put down our differences and focus on what we share, we find joy and peace. And that's better than a trophy.

Coach's tip: Have the players do an intense activity or tournament and monitor how they treat each other. Remind them that they are on the same team and that unity is more important than winning the activity.

Coach's Tip-of-the-Day

The day or two before a game, many coaches ease up on the conditioning aspect of practice and focus on things such as set pieces and corner kicks. Some coaches find it useful to work on these things in a scrimmage setting. In the normal flow of a scrimmage, the coach may stop play and instruct the players to do an "indirect free-kick" to allow both the offense and defense to practice the plays on the fly. Sometimes, two or three repetitions while play is stopped are also helpful.

Player's Tip-of-the-Day

Starting to drink water the night before a game is important. Your body needs to begin the hydration process early enough so that the muscles are prepared for the game.

For more information about today's guest writer, John Spracklin, log on to beyondsoccer.org.

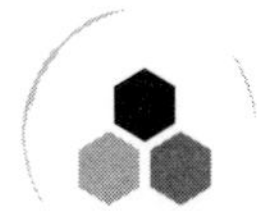

The Front Yard Goal

1 Chronicles 28:9 *"And you, my son Solomon, acknowledge the God of your father, and serve him with wholehearted devotion and with a willing mind, for the LORD searches every heart and understands every motive behind the thoughts. If you seek him, he will be found by you; but if you forsake him, he will reject you forever."*

Growing up, we had a soccer goal in our front yard that became a landmark for where we lived. All you had to say was, "We live in the house on Jefferson Boulevard with the soccer goal in the front yard," and inevitably the person would know exactly where it was. It was a perfect goal. The posts, which were from an old clothesline we had lying around, were firmly secured in the ground, the cross-bar was exactly 24 feet long, and there were supports that projected from the top corners to help frame the net. The style of the nets in the most recent World Cup determined how we hung the net: straight down, box-shaped, down at an angle or so tight the ball bounced right back.

If you seek him, he will be found by you.

I can remember riding home on the school bus thinking about how badly I just wanted to get out there and shoot on goal. My brother would normally agree to play goalie, but if not, I'd recruit other family members or neighbors. A constant stream of people beeping their horns filled the air, as friends, classmates and other soccer fans happened by to say hello. After about an hour, the recruited goalie normally had enough, while some of the same cars that passed earlier would shorten their beep as if to say "You're still out here?" I had a passion for the game of soccer. I wanted to get better and play professionally someday. God calls us to practice every day as well. In spending time in prayer, reading His Word and going to Church, we develop the skills to help us build our faith. But it takes discipline, much like it takes discipline for an athlete to become a better player. I oftentimes pray that God will "quicken my mind" to remind me that I need to regularly seek Him. Ask God to quicken your mind this week and periodically in your life. He understands our busy schedules and knows our hearts, but He also requires us to make time for Him.

Coach's Tip-of-the-Day

Shooting competitions can create an atmosphere of fun and pressure. Place two goals facing one another about 40 to 50 yards apart with goalkeepers in each. Split the team into two groups and position them on opposite goals and the opposite posts. Coaches or volunteers stand at the midway point laying off wall passes to the shooters. Once a player has shot the ball, the next person in line can go. Both teams begin at the same time and shoot for three minutes, trying to accumulate more goals than the other team. The losers are given push-ups or sit-ups to instill added stake in winning the game.

Player's Tip-of-the-Day

Here are a few games you can play if there are only two or three of you shooting on a goal:

Rapid Fire – The object is to scatter the balls around and shoot all of them as quickly as you can. This helps develop unconscious shooting as you try to place balls in different places in the goal.

Two Touch – The goalie drives or punts a challenging ball out and you are forced to take a controlling touch and then shoot quickly with your second touch.

Goalie/Shooter Challenge – Everyone hates chasing the balls, so you make a deal with the goalie that if you score 4 or more out of 10 balls, the goalie chases the balls; less than 4, the shooter chases the balls. Also, the shooter continues to shoot until all balls are out-of-play completely. Balls that score or are saved by the keeper are still eligible to shoot with. By concentrating on keeping the ball on goal, the shooter develops good habits of keeping the ball low and under control, not wasting shots by hitting over the goal.

The Terrible Little Tongue

by Steve DeCou, College Soccer Coach

Psalm 141:3 *Set a guard over my mouth, O Lord; keep watch over the door of my lips.*

The game is tied, you receive the ball at the top of the box and after beating your defender you fire a shot...wide. When it happens, your tongue gets you in trouble. You didn't mean to say it but you did. And the referee has only one option, to show you the yellow card. While the offense has been dealt with, what has this done to your testimony with coaches, teammates and opponents? Even more importantly, what has it done to your relationship with Christ? Being a college head coach, I am not immune to slips of the tongue. On many occasions I've had to ask forgiveness for things I've said.

> *Set a guard over my mouth, O Lord; keep watch over the door of my lips.*

Take heart, though, because man has been struggling for thousands of years to control what comes out of his mouth. David in the above verse is asking God to help him with what he says because he can't control his own tongue. If a man of David's spiritual stature had problems with what he said, how can we expect to be any different? If your tongue is getting you in trouble, do as David did and take it to the Lord, asking for His help with the matter. Find someone who will help hold you accountable and be there for counsel, whether that be a coach, teammate or friend.

Coach's Tip-of-the-Day

"The game is the greatest teacher" - This was a point of emphasis in a coaching course that I took. Drills and small-sided games are great and much needed, but get your team scrimmaging for at least half of your training session. Limitations and restrictions can be placed on the scrimmage, but the more touches your players have in game-like situations the more they will understand what you are trying to teach.

Player's Tip-of-the-Day

Looking for an easy way to improve your touch and comfort on the ball? Juggle. Learning to use different aspects of the body to control the ball will help you be comfortable with the ball, and the more comfortable you are with the ball the easier the game will become. Work at increasing the number of times you can keep the ball up, and then try to incorporate other parts of the body (i.e., feet, knees, head). Also, don't forget that God gave you both a left and a right.

For more information about today's guest writer, Steve DeCou, log on to beyondsoccer.org.

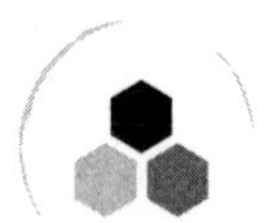

Soccer Parents

Deuteronomy 11: 18-19 *Fix these words of mine in your hearts and minds; tie them as symbols on your hands and bind them on your foreheads. Teach them to your children, talking about them when you sit at home and when you walk along the road, when you lie down and when you get up.*

There was an article a few years ago about a youth soccer league that mandated a rule that said anyone on the sidelines, including parents, could be yellow carded for yelling anything but praise to the players and coaches. Friends and family were allowed to encourage and praise or were asked to say nothing at all. As you can imagine, the results were overwhelmingly positive. Kids came off the field with high self-esteem, and parents learned to change their responses and act appropriately.

Seeing that their parents are living as Christians is what kids need to see.

In a culture where kids are constantly being pulled the other direction, parents need to constantly remind themselves that love, encouraging words and bringing up their children with godly principles is so important. Seeing that their parents are living as Christians is what kids need to see, not just hearing Bible stories in Sunday school. Are you setting a good Christian example for your children? In the car on the way home from the games, do you bicker or perhaps gossip about other people or talk about what a great job certain players did? Do you bash the referees or talk about respect for authority? Do you grumble about the coach's decisions or do you show appreciation that he or she takes the time to invest in the lives of youth, and specifically your child?

I had an opportunity to referee U-8 recreational soccer games for kids one summer as part of a job description. Managed by a Christian organization, this league required that before starting the game, I bring both teams, coaches and all participants to the center circle to introduce myself and say a prayer over the game. What a concept for all those little children to experience: everyone humbling themselves before Christ, not caring for a moment about what car they drive, the designer shoes they wore or where they'll eat lunch later, just asking God to keep watch over a simple game and help them compete in a Christian manner. In the game of life, don't just teach your kids how to live, but as their teammate, show them what it means to win.

Coach's Tip-of-the-Day

Confrontation is unfortunately an inevitable part of being a coach. When confronted by angry parents, keep your cool and offer to talk further later that day or on the phone. Many coaches find that a pre-season talk with all the parents is an effective way to get coaches and parents on the same page on topics such as this one.

Player's Tip-of-the-Day

Take a moment the next chance you get to express your appreciation to the coach who helps your team. A simple thank-you note, e-mail or gift certificate would go a long way.

Don't Let the Good Crowd Out the Best

by Mark Steffens, Professional Soccer Coach

Luke 10:38-42 *As Jesus and his disciples were on their way, he came to a village where a woman named Martha opened her home to him. She had a sister called Mary, who sat at the Lord's feet listening to what he said. But Martha was distracted by all the preparations that had to be made. She came to him and asked, "Lord, don't you care that my sister has left me to do the work by myself? Tell her to help me!" "Martha, Martha," the Lord answered, "you are worried and upset about many things, but only one thing is needed. Mary has chosen what is better, and it will not be taken away from her."*

Often we get so wrapped up in doing good things that we lose sight of what is best. This is perfectly illustrated in the gospel of Luke when Jesus visits Mary and her sister Martha. Martha wanted to have everything just perfect for her friend Jesus. She made all the preparations for her company: cooking the food, setting the table, straightening the house, etc. In contrast, Mary sat at Jesus' feet and listened to Him. All the good things that Martha did were important; the problem was that she was so very busy doing all that stuff that she missed out on what was most important… sitting at Jesus' feet, building her relationship with Christ. Sounds familiar, doesn't it. We get so caught up in well doing that we forget to spend time at Jesus' feet. In verse 42, when Jesus said *"only one thing is needed,"* He was referring to spending time alone with God and getting to know Him better! Just being still before God and listening to His "still small voice" is vital for our spiritual growth. We need to be reminded every day to put our

> *We get so caught up in well doing that we forget to spend time at Jesus' feet.*

busyness aside and not be distracted from our goal of spiritual maturity by sitting at the Master's feet.

Coach's Tip-of-the-Day

Hand ball is a fun warm-up to mix things up at practice. Break the group up into two even teams with regular size goals and a shortened field. Players must throw or kick the ball to their teammates without letting the ball hit the ground. If the ball does hit the ground, it's turned over to the other team. Players only have five seconds or five steps, whichever comes first, to get rid of the ball. A violation of this rule results in a turnover as well. Furthermore, players can only score by heading the ball into the goal. This warm-up often becomes fast paced and high scoring, and players have fun doing something a little different for a change. From a soccer perspective, this game can also help players learn to pass and move to keep possession of the ball. This reasoning will also help parents understand when they are wondering why their son or daughter is throwing a ball at soccer practice!

Player's Tip-of-the-Day

Wet conditions can cause leather cleats to get waterlogged. A simple trick is to stuff newspapers into the shoes to help absorb the water.

For more information about today's guest writer, Mark Steffens, log on to beyondsoccer.org.

Challenge Each Other

Proverbs 27:17 *As iron sharpens iron, so one man sharpens another.*

One of the most important concepts to realize in the game of soccer is that players must practice against other players who possess equal or more advanced skills in order to become better and take their game to the next level. Soccer is a game of ongoing creativity, ball control, quick thinking, precision passing and so much more. In order for an individual or a team to develop skills like this, hours of training in a "challenging atmosphere" is required. There are no magic drills that will make a team come together or allow a player to develop on-field brilliance rather, it is the competitive, game-like situations that the players need to face on a daily basis in order to improve. A coach's role is to create this environment while offering encouragement and passionately selling his or her tactics and agenda in every practice. The players' responsibility is to take advantage of the times when they are challenged on the practice field, focusing on their game and working to raise their level.

As the iron is sharpened in us, we are then more equipped to take the message of Christ into the real world.

Much is the same in our Christian walk. If we immerse ourselves in an environment of Christian love and encouragement, we are bound to develop our faith and become closer to God. Other Christians bring to us unique perspectives on life, a greater range of biblical knowledge and a myriad of different experiences. When we tap into those sources of insight, the result over time is an improvement in ourselves and in those around us. As the iron is sharpened in us, we are then more equipped to take the message of Christ into the real world. With quiet confidence we approach each day like the start of a game, knowing we have surrounded our lives with the best of the best, learned from those around us and equipped ourselves with the knowledge that will help us be successful in pursuit of the ultimate goal.

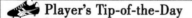

Coach's Tip-of-the-Day

Small-sided games are an important part of any soccer practice. When players can take more touches on the ball in a tight space, they are forced to make decisions and develop the skills needed in a real game. There are a variety of small-sided games to choose from. Sometimes it is useful to play six versus six with a shortened field using regular size goals with the goalkeepers. Other times the team can be split up into smaller groups of four versus four, for example. In this case, cones can be used for the goals without having a designated goalkeeper. For younger players, it is often helpful to place an arc around the front of the goal, "no-man's-land," where players are not allowed to enter. This helps solve the problem of one player staying back as the goalkeeper, forcing everyone to be involved in the field play.
See a diagram of this drill at beyondsoccer.org.

Player's Tip-of-the-Day

During that time in practice when you have the opportunity to play in small-sided games or scrimmages, raise your level of awareness, focus and work on things that you know you may need to work on. At one point in my career, I had a mental list of things that I wanted to improve on: quicker decisions, better first touch and keeping my head on a swivel. By focusing on the things that you consider a weakness, you will quickly find that your game improves and your confidence increases.

Contentment

1 Timothy 6:6 *But godliness with* **contentment** *is great gain.*

Our professional indoor league had undergone some downsizing one season, and as a result, we acquired some high-caliber players from other teams. As a younger player, my playing time decreased that year and I was sent to the back of the line to wait my turn…again!

God calls us to be content in all circumstances.

In the middle of the season, I was asked to do a radio interview to promote Christian Youth Night, an upcoming soccer game and postgame Christian concert. I was up earlier than usual that morning and made the trip into the city. Struggling to wake up and not yet having had a coherent conversation with anyone, I was hustled into the station and was shown my place to sit behind the microphone, while the announcers nodded to me as they finished up the traffic report and weather forecast. Within moments, I was introduced and asked the question "Is it difficult to not be playing on a regular basis, like you did last season?" The question caught me off guard. I had expected to answer general questions about how our team was doing, about our upcoming games, and other such typical interview questions. I paused, stumbled over my words a bit, and said, "Yes, it is difficult to not play on a regular basis. You train so hard and have invested so much time and energy, it's hard to not have an opportunity to play on the weekends."

I learned a lot that season and began to realize that God calls us to be content in all circumstances—when things are going great and when we're struggling.

You may have deserved that promotion you didn't get, you may not have gotten that sale you worked so hard for or may not have made the team you tried out for, but God has a reason for everything. He asks us to keep our eyes focused on Him and trust His plan for our lives…to be content…to keep working hard.

In this life, all we can do is give our best and leave the rest up to God.

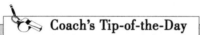

Coach's Tip-of-the-Day

The best thing a coach can do is be up front and honest with players about their role on the team. If there is a player who doesn't get much playing time or who obviously is struggling with a lack of confidence, take time to encourage and work with that player one-on-one. Young or old, a coach can have a great impact on the personal growth of a person beyond the soccer playing field.

Player's Tip-of-the-Day

Spending time on the bench is a hard thing for any player to do, but the world of sports is full of stories of persistence that pay off. If your current position on the team is not playing a lot lately, keep working hard and put soccer in the right perspective.

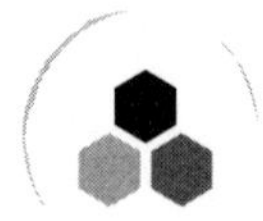

The Goal of Our Instruction

by Ed Meadors, College Soccer Coach

Philippians 3:13-14 *Brothers, I do not consider myself yet to have taken hold of it. But one thing I do: Forgetting what is behind and straining toward what is ahead, I press on toward the goal to win the prize for which God has called me heavenward in Christ Jesus.*
1 Timothy 1:5 *The goal of this command is love, which comes from a pure heart and a good conscience and a sincere faith.*

An "own goal" in soccer occurs when a player mistakenly scores on the team's own goal rather than their opponents'. Those like myself who have scored "own goals" know the painful embarrassment associated with this tragic mistake. It's the soccer player's worst nightmare. The same holds true for the exercise of the Christian life. In confusing goals, we risk devoting our energy to accomplish things that often do not contribute to the Kingdom of God, and sometimes are even harmful to it. This being the case, what are the goals that the Bible instructs Christians to aggressively shoot for? Two passages immediately come to mind. First, in Philippians Paul writes, *"Forgetting what is behind and straining toward what is ahead, I press on toward the goal to win the prize for which God has called heavenward in Christ Jesus"* (Philippians 3:13-14). Paul explains with these words that his ultimate goal is to experience eternity with God and the resurrected Christ. As he progressed on his missionary journeys, his motivation for enduring persecution and hardship was his knowledge that each step led him closer to his inheritance of eternal life with God, as made possible by Jesus' death and resurrection. The second passage that comes to

We risk devoting our energy to accomplish things that often do not contribute to the Kingdom of God.

mind is 1 Timothy 1:5: *"But the goal of this command is love, which comes from a pure heart and a good conscience and a sincere faith."* This means that the objective of our efforts, as followers of Christ, is to encourage and teach others to model sacrificial love, which in turn is to model genuine Christ-likeness. Our striving should always be motivated by this goal. When programs, projects, performances and other endeavors (even success in soccer!) cloud our vision of this goal, we inevitably miss the mark. And when we define ultimate success as the accomplishment of these substitute endeavors, we run the risk of scoring for the enemy and not for our King.

Coach's Tip-of-the-Day

Take time to discuss with players how to avoid the danger of "own goals." A simple drill that requires players to pass back to the keeper to the right or left of the goal mouth helps train players to eliminate the risk. Also important is discussion of what to do when under stress in the penalty box. The old adage "When in doubt kick it out" may be ugly, but it is still often the wise course of action.

Player's Tip-of-the-Day

Target Practice: When shooting on goal it's often helpful to have visual aids to use as targets. A T-shirt spread out and hung in the corners makes for a target hanging from the top. Cones can also be placed 4 or 5 feet in from the post on the line to separate the goal into three sections. As a shooter, pick a side or a corner before shooting and then develop your skills with repetition to place the ball into the desired section. Over time, hopefully you will be able to unconsciously find the open spot in the goal during the games.
See a diagram of this drill at beyondsoccer.org.

For more information about today's guest writer, Ed Meadors, log on to beyondsoccer.org.

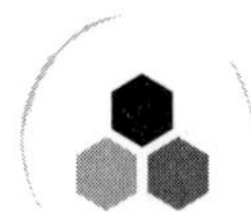

The Goalkeeper

Ephesians 6:11-18 *Put on the full armor of God so that you can take your stand against the devil's schemes. Stand firm then, with the belt of truth buckled around your waist, with the breastplate of righteousness in place, and with your feet fitted with the readiness that comes from the gospel of peace. In addition to all this, take up the shield of faith, with which you can extinguish all the flaming arrows of the evil one. Take the helmet of salvation and the sword of the Spirit, which is the word of God. And pray in the Spirit on all occasions with all kinds of prayers and requests. With this in mind, be alert and always keep on praying for all the saints.*

On a soccer team, the goalkeeper is the last line of defense, doing whatever it takes to keep the other team from scoring. Normally clothed with more protective gear, the goalkeeper stands out among the other team members with his or her gloves, padded pants and a colorful, long-sleeve shirt. Many keepers are asked to be the leader of their defense, directing the field players in front of them to mark-up and organize things on corner kicks and free kicks. Some keepers have the ability to make spectacular, diving saves, while some have an uncanny ability to defuse the play by smothering the ball at the top of the 18-yard box. Other keepers, like Mexico's Jorge Campos, have their own style and flair all together. Campos is so active and unorthodox that he oftentimes gets involved in the offense throughout the course of the game, dribbling out of pressure in the back and continuing on into the midfield. Mexican fans have learned they can never predict what Campos will do next. No matter what style a keeper possesses, however, his or her job is simple: keep the ball

Put on the full armor of God.

out of the goal. This position can carry with it extreme pressure, as keepers contemplate their every action, knowing that one lapse could result in a score by the other team. Paul reminds us in this passage that each day we need to *"put on the full armor of God"* so we can protect ourselves from an evil world. Our lives can become bombarded with shots to our confidence, temptations, doubt, insecurity, failures and so much more, but Paul describes how the armor of God can offer us *"truth," "peace," "faith"* and *"salvation."* Furthermore, if we don't take the time to *"pray always"* and prepare our minds for these opponents, we can fall victim to discouragement and failure. God will never cause you to face something you can't handle. During those times when the other team seems to have momentum and you are struggling to stay in the game, remember that God will protect you and help you through those tough times.

Coach's Tip-of-the-Day

Goalie Wars is a fun, challenging game for keepers to play in practice. The goals are moved about 30 yards apart (more or less depending on the age of the players), facing each other, with a keeper in each goal. One goalie starts with the ball and tries to kick, throw or drop-kick the ball past the other keeper into the opposite goal. The action goes back and forth until one of the keepers scores 5 goals. Keepers will be able to work on making saves, as well as on throwing and kicking accuracy. They will also receive a good cardiovascular workout and learn to perform when they are tired.

See a diagram of this drill at beyondsoccer.org.

Player's Tip-of-the-Day

As a goalkeeper, it is important to take charge on the field. With the ability to use your hands, you are in a unique position. Yelling "keeper!" when going up for a high ball, for example, can help make your teammates aware of your position, allowing you to go get the ball in less traffic. Directing defenders and midfielders to mark-up the other team's players can help organize things quickly. Keep in mind that you are facing the play, which means that everything is in front of you. This gives you the best perspective of anyone on the field.

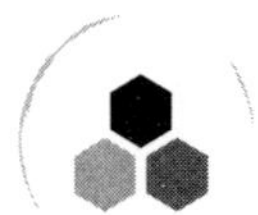

Gut Feeling

Proverbs 19:21 *Many are the plans in a man's heart, but it is the LORD's purpose that prevails.*

The U.S. Women's National team won the 1999 World Cup in dramatic fashion, beating Brazil in penalty kicks that summer. Who can forget the image of Brandi Chastain celebrating her game-winning goal on the fifth and final shot of the penalty kicks? While the country celebrated in that moment, Brandi suddenly became an icon in the sports world and her life would never again be the same.

Jesus chose ordinary people as His disciples to do His work.

Tony DiCicco, coach of the U.S. team, surprisingly enough did not choose Brandi initially to take that kick. Moments before Coach DiCicco was scheduled to turn in his penalty kick list to the referees, he had a gut feeling and replaced Julie Foudy with Brandi for the fifth spot on the list. The rest, as they say, is history.

Jesus chose ordinary people as His disciples to do His work, a list of men that some may have questioned, but He had a gut feeling about them. These men, as we know it, changed the face of Christianity forever. Although their lives from the world's perspective may have seemed ordinary, their purpose in life turned out to be world changing.

The Lord also has a purpose for your life if you take time to pray for His direction and submit to His plans. He has a "gut feeling" about you.

Coach's Tip-of-the-Day

When doing sprints with your team, instruct players to start off in different positions. On the starting line, have players start lying on their stomachs, on their knees, in Indian-style, standing sideways or standing backwards. This will develop quickness and agility. Much of soccer is not running straight ahead, but rather changing directions constantly.

Player's Tip-of-the-Day

Keeping your head on a swivel is a good habit to develop and one that will cause you to become a better player. This means constantly taking a look around you to help you decide what to do next. Especially when the ball is traveling towards you, take a quick look over your shoulder or around you to size up the situation. At the higher levels, your time and space decreases, forcing you to make quick decisions on the ball. In practice and when doing simple passing drills, work on developing this into your game. As it becomes habit, you will find yourself making better decisions and gaining confidence.

Using Your *Feet*!

by John Stayskal, Ultimate Goal Ministries

Romans 10:15 *And how can they preach unless they are sent? As it is written, "How beautiful are the feet of those who bring good news!"*[1]

Is there anything more rewarding than bringing the Good News to someone and leading that one in following Christ? If you have ever been directly involved in someone's decision to follow Christ, you know the answer.

How can you effectively bring the Good News to someone? You're probably not a Billy Graham (believe me, I'm not even close). Here is my suggestion: Use your *feet*! Use soccer.

> *Make it your mission field as well, and use your* feet *as a tool to bring the Good News to someone.*

Romans 10:15 refers to actively taking the Gospel to someone, the same concept as in Matthew 28 where Jesus tells us to *go*!

Obviously soccer wasn't even a sport in Paul's day, so I'm sure he wasn't referring to the sport. But why can't you literally use your feet to take the Good News to people? It's definitely one way of actively taking the Gospel to someone.

Finding a common interest is one of the first steps to building relationships. One of my greatest interests is soccer, as it is for many in the world. Someone once said of the soccer-playing world, "For them, soccer isn't a matter of life and death...it's more important than that."

What better way is there for you to build a relationship with someone than playing soccer together?

You can start a soccer-themed seekers' Bible study for your team. Go on a soccer mission trip. Help organize a neighborhood clinic. Work a soccer camp. Start a weekly pick up game. Ask to play with a multiethnic team playing in your area. Be creative. All you need is a soccer ball and your *feet*.

Our ministries mission statement is simply "making the soccer field our mission field." Make it your mission field as well and use your *feet* as a tool to bring the Good News to someone.

Coach's Tip-of-the-Day

Knock Out: This is a game primarily for youth players that can help them develop dribbling and shielding skills. Each Player has a ball and dribbles around in a grid approximately 20 yards x 20 yards, depending on the number of kids. The players are instructed to try to kick the other players' balls out, while keeping control of their own balls. If a player's ball is knocked out or dribbles accidentally out of the grid, the player must sit outside and wait until the next game. Keep a close eye that players do not foul other players when going for the ball, to maintain a safe environment.

Player's Tip-of-the-Day

Partner juggling is a challenging exercise that can help develop touch on the ball. With a partner, keep the ball up in the air with all parts of your body. Before transferring the ball to your partner in the air, call out a number from one to ten. The partner receiving the ball must juggle the exact amount of times called out and then transfer the ball back, calling out a number while the ball is in the air. The play goes back and forth until a mistake is made.

For more information about today's guest writer, John Stayskal, log on to beyondsoccer.org.

The Shot Heard Round the World

Psalm 107: 23-30 *Others went out on the sea in ships; they were merchants on the mighty waters. They saw the works of the Lord, his wonderful deeds in the deep. For he spoke and stirred up a tempest that lifted high the waves. They mounted up to the heavens and went down to the depths; in their peril their courage melted away. They reeled and staggered like drunken men; they were at their wits' end. Then they cried out to the Lord in their trouble, and he brought them out of their distress. He stilled the storm to a whisper; the waves of the sea were hushed. They were glad when it grew calm, and he guided them to their desired haven.*

In the final World Cup qualifying game for the United States in 1990, Paul Caligiuri scored a goal that became known as "The Shot Heard Round the World." It was the game-winning goal that sent the U.S. to the World Cup for the first time in forty years.

As a defender, Paul's play was always steady and consistent, allowing him to play in 110 games for the red, white and blue throughout his career.

Great players find a way to win. They score goals or come up with big saves when the game is on the line. They do so with a controlled intensity, quiet confidence and calmness in the thick of battle.

As believers we should approach each day knowing that God is in control.

As believers we should approach each day knowing that God is in control, guiding us to our *"desired haven."* Reflect on your life. Do you approach each day with a quiet confidence and inner peace? If not, begin developing the habit of spending time with God on a deeper level. The blessings and refocusing that result will become life-changing.

Coach's Tip-of-the-Day

Competition in practice should often be a rule of thumb when coaches are developing their practice agendas. Mental toughness is developed when something is at stake in the exercise. Players have an incentive to, hopefully, raise their level and reduce their mistakes. Youth coaches may opt to have the losers do silly animal exercises, while coaches of higher levels may find that push-ups or extra sprints generate intensity.

Player's Tip-of-the-Day

Want the ball! Good soccer players want to get the ball so they can make something happen. Don't be content with just playing your role. Ask for the ball and create opportunities for your team to advance the ball up the field and create scoring opportunities. This all starts in practice. Get in the habit of wanting the ball in practice and don't be afraid to lose it. Try things. The only way to get better is to work hard each day on your skills and develop confidence in your abilities.

Press On!

by Steve Wagner, Professional Soccer Chaplain

Philipians 3:12-14 *Not that I have already obtained all this, or have already been made perfect, but I press on to take hold of that for which Christ Jesus took hold of me. Brothers, I do not consider myself yet to have taken hold of it. But one thing I do: Forgetting what is behind and straining toward what is ahead, I press on toward the goal to win the prize for which God has called me heavenward in Christ Jesus.*

Shortly after World War II, the great British prime minister, Winston Churchill, was invited to address the graduating class of one of England's most prestigious universities. Churchill walked to the speaker's podium, looked straight into the eyes of the graduating students, and gave the following speech:

"Never, never, never, never, never, never give up!"

The Apostle Paul wrote a similar thought: *"I press on."* No matter how difficult the circumstances, no matter how hard the task, no matter how great the challenge, "I press on." In other words, I never give up on God.

Never, never, never, never, never, never give up!

How do you stay strong in your faith in God and trust in Jesus Christ when life is tough? Here's what Philippians chapter three instructs:

1. *"Forgetting what is behind."* In other words, the past is past. You can't live wrapped up in yesterday's regrets or yesterday's successes and be at your best for today. Life is not intended to be defined by your failures or your nostalgia. Life is meant to be defined by knowing Jesus

Christ and His purpose for your life.

2. *"Straining toward what is ahead."* Jesus spoke of loving God *"with all your heart and with all your soul and with all your mind and with all your strength"* (see Mark 12:30). In other words, regardless of your circumstances, your devotion belongs to God.

Lance Armstrong, the great Tour de France bicycle champion, once commented that the race is won and lost when the competitors are pedaling uphill. Concerning Christ, you are who you are when you are pedaling uphill.

3. *"I press on toward the goal."* This means allowing no distractions concerning having Jesus Christ as the focus of your life.

I know a young mother whose child was dying of cancer. The night before he died, the child was hallucinating and quite scared. To calm her son, this mom told him, "When you see Jesus, run to Him."

That's an incredible word for any moment in life. "Run to Jesus." Never give up on Him!

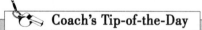

Coach's Tip-of-the-Day

Interrupting practice too much is a tendency that some coaches get caught up in and can inhibit the rhythm of a scrimmage or drill. Take notes and try pointing out things during a water break instead.

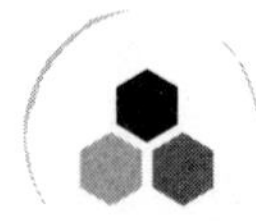

Player's Tip-of-the-Day

Mental toughness is developed when players learn to forget their mistakes on the field and focus on the next play. If you carry mistakes with you throughout that game and future games, you will find that you struggle to find your confidence and your personal performance will struggle. Don't get caught up in the game of keeping track of how many mistakes you made and how many good plays you made. This only leads to a mental war in your mind, taking your focus off of the game. Remember, everyone makes mistakes, even the top players in the world.

For more information about today's guest writer, Steve Wagner, log on to beyondsoccer.org.

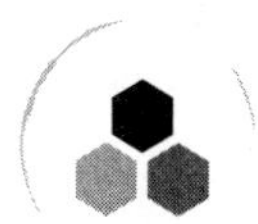

Momentum

Psalm 46:1-4 *God is our refuge and strength, an ever-present help in trouble. Therefore we will not fear, though the earth give way and the mountains fall into the heart of the sea, though its waters roar and foam and the mountains quake with their surging. Selah. There is a river whose streams make glad the city of God, the holy place where the Most High dwells.*

Momentum is often a factor during the course of a soccer match. A team gains possession at midfield and strings together a series of nice passes, the winger beats his defender and crosses a low-driven ball, an outstretched team-mate meets the ball with a diving header, the ball glances off the side post. A keeper stands flat-footed, dazed by the sequence of events. Momentum has shifted. As play begins again, much of the same continues as the offense relentlessly "knocks at the door" – shots are fired, crosses are coming in and the defense, in desperation, continues to clear the ball.

Go to a quiet place, your refuge, and have a chat with God.

I vividly remember telling my wife one day that it felt like "everyone was against me." It was a time many can probably relate to, when I simply felt like I was losing the game. Life's challenges seemed to be getting the best of me. Ever feel that way? Well, if you do, there's a tactic that can help. Go to a quiet place, your refuge, and have a chat with God.

Coach's Tip-of-the-Day

Dribbling through cones is a simple and effective drill for youth coaches. To instill some fun and competition, try incorporating this drill into a relay format. Separate the team into two or three groups with a line of cones for each. Variations can also be applied for future rounds, e.g., right foot only on the way up and left only on the way back.

Player's Tip-of-the-Day

Every striker or offensive player goes through a scoring drought when you "just can't seem to find the back of the net." Oftentimes this is caused by an unrealized change in your shooting technique. Take a minute to shoot the ball in slow motion, focusing on your plant foot and on where your foot makes contact with the ball. Notice also where your shooting foot ends up. If you've been shooting the ball high, you'll probably notice your plant foot is behind the ball and you are leaning back. If you are shooting the ball to the left more than normal, you'll probably notice your plant foot is pointing too far in that direction and you're striking the ball with the inside more so than the laces. Once diagnosed, now start striking some shots at half speed with the adjustments in mind and build up to 100%. Repetition like this for the next couple of days after practice can hopefully start to solve the problem.

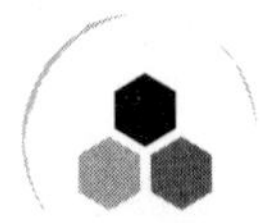

Giving Up My Rights

by Paul Shedd, Soccer Coach/Ministry Director

Galatians 2:20 *I have been crucified with Christ and I no longer live, but Christ lives in me. The life I live in the body, I live by faith in the Son of God, who loved me and gave himself for me.*

As soccer players and coaches, we often think we have certain rights. My right to defend myself verbally and physically, my right to have a well-officiated game, my right to have the ball when and where I want it are some of these. The following short anecdote may help us understand what rights we really do have as Christians.

As followers of Christ when we play and coach, it is important that we give God our rights.

A missionary in Dutch New Guinea years ago planted some pineapple plants in the hope that as these plants ripened he and his wife would enjoy them. However, as they became edible, he noticed that the nationals were stealing them. He tried several different approaches to deter the theft. These included closing the clinic, shutting the store, and buying a German shepherd. But all attempts were in vain—the pineapples kept disappearing!

While on furlough, he attended a Christian seminar that encouraged him to give up his rights and turn them over to God—even the rights to his pineapples! Upon returning to the mission field, he knelt by the plants and gave them to God. The disappearing of the fruit no longer infuriated him. The nationals came up to him one day and said, "Tou-wan (foreigner), you are now a Christian." This statement surprised him!

They then went on to tell him that instead of just telling them to love each other, he was actually loving them. As a result of the missionary giving up his pineapple gardens, many came to Christ.

The Apostle Paul understood what rights he had when he stated that he was crucified—he had the rights of a dead man—none. As followers of Christ when we play and coach, it is important that we give God our rights. It is then that He will be glorified through our hard and fair play!

Coach's Tip-of-the-Day

A simple but forgotten aspect of the game is to play the way you face. Top-level teams do this all the time. Playing the way you face has two advantages: It keeps the ball moving rapidly, and the person receiving the ball usually will see more options. A simple warm-up drill is to have all the players in a 20 x 30 yard grid moving, passing one touch with one ball. Throw in an additional ball as they get better at it.

Player's Tip-of-the-Day

As you approach each game and each practice, commit your rights to God. It will make you a better team player!

For more information about today's guest writer, Paul Shedd, log on to beyondsoccer.org.

Foul!

Proverbs 16:18 *Pride goes before destruction, a haughty spirit before a fall.*

Soccer is a sport that can cause us to reach the full spectrum of emotion in the blink of an eye. Goal scoring causes passionate celebrations. Some players fall to their knees, fists clinched, while others take off soaring across the field with their arms open. The goalkeeper, however, stands motionless. A look of despair and defeat is on his face as he turns to see the ball tucked in the goal behind him. During the course of play, emotions can also play a big part. If we're not careful, our reactions to these emotions can have consequences on and off the field.

I was playing in an adult recreational soccer league one summer to work on my fitness level and get some touches on the ball. My reputation was one of a former successful college player who'd recently had stints with some outdoor professional teams. Knowing this, I was out to prove myself. What should have been a humble, Christ-like spirit in me that day was now nothing but pride.

It's not what we say that witnesses to others, but rather what we do.

I began to read a play in the middle of the field and picked up my pace to a sprint. As the opponent turned with the ball, I quickly intercepted and began breaking for our goal. Next thing I knew, someone made a sliding tackle from the side that met the ball along with my right ankle. Crashing to the ground, I bounced up, got in his face and proceeded to tell him off without a moment's notice. Needless to say I received a yellow card and was sent off the field embarrassed, but more importantly I lost an opportunity to witness to anyone within shouting distance of that field.

When you get caught up in the emotion of life, remember that oftentimes it's not what we say that witnesses to others, but rather what we do and how we react to the circumstances we find ourselves in. People perceive you to be different when you walk out the Christian life. Prove them right by keeping your emotions in check so you don't run the risk of regretting your actions later.

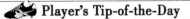

Coach's Tip-of-the-Day

Slide tackling is a difficult technique to coach with a specific drill at practice, but challenge your players to keep their eyes on the ball, while staying in control of their bodies. A hard tackle will oftentimes draw a foul or a yellow card, but a well-timed tackle that seems intended for the ball can be successful and help a team gain possession. Coaches should also explain that slide tackling from behind is strictly prohibited. Furthermore, some leagues prohibit all slide tackling at the younger levels for safety reasons. Check with your league rulebook for clarification.

Player's Tip-of-the-Day

Slide tackling is normally a skill that is developed over time in game-like situations and is more about timing than anything else. Keep in mind also where you are on the field before committing to a slide tackle. If you leave your feet, the attacking player could gain an advantage if you miss and he or she dribbles around you. Oftentimes, slide tackling is used in desperation. More times than not, applying good defensive pressure on the ball to slow play down is more effective.

Do What You Can

by Scott Taylor, Brilla Soccer Ministries

Matthew 28:19-20 *"Therefore go and make disciples of all nations, baptizing them in the name of the Father and of the Son and of the Holy Spirit, and teaching them to obey everything I have commanded you. And surely I am with you always, to the very end of the age."*
Mark 14: 3-9 *While he was in Bethany, reclining at the table in the home of a man known as Simon the Leper, a woman came with an alabaster jar of very expensive perfume, made of pure nard. She broke the jar and poured the perfume on his head. Some of those present were saying indignantly to one another, "Why this waste of perfume? It could have been sold for more than a year's wages and the money given to the poor." And they rebuked her harshly. "Leave her alone," said Jesus. "Why are you bothering her? She has done a beautiful thing to me. The poor you will always have with you, and you can help them any time you want. But you will not always have me. She did what she could. She poured perfume on my body beforehand to prepare for my burial. I tell you the truth, wherever the gospel is preached throughout the world, what she has done will also be told, in memory of her."*

Oftentimes, people react to the Great Commission feeling that they can't be effective witnesses for Jesus because they aren't great leaders or speakers. I have found myself thinking this way at times as well. Sometimes when I start talking, my words get all mixed up and I get nervous. I often think, "Why would anyone listen to me?" Recently, I read a story in the Bible about a person who could have the same problem that I have. It was a woman who might have been thinking, "What could I possibly give Jesus? No one will listen to me because I am nothing, worthless. I am a terrible person."

Fortunately, she found something she could give Jesus.

This woman had no special skills that we know of. She was probably not a great leader, or she may even have had a bad reputation. All she had was a bottle of perfume. So, she gave that to Jesus. He was pleased with her offering because, as He said, “She did what she could.”

But after that He said, “Wherever the gospel is preached throughout the world, what she has done will also be told. . . .” She wasn’t trying to get fame or glory for herself; she was just trying to glorify Jesus. Because she gave what she could to Jesus, many people have heard and will hear her story and come to know Jesus.

I hope that Jesus says the same thing about me, “He is doing what he can.”

I am not a great speaker. I am not a great leader. One of the few things that I have is the ability to play soccer. So I will give that to Jesus. He has given it to me for a reason, and I believe that reason is to give it back to Him by sharing with others while I play soccer.

One of the few things that I have is the ability to play soccer. So I will give that to Jesus.

What are you giving Jesus? Are you doing what you can? Do you have a special skill that He has given you? Can you play a sport very well? Can you sing or play an instrument? Are you an artist? Do you have friends or family who look up to you? Is there anything that you have that you can use for Jesus? If you can’t find anything, you need to keep looking. Jesus has given each one of us something that we can use to share with others about Him.

All Jesus asks of us is that we do what we can.

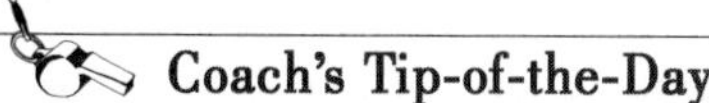

Coach's Tip-of-the-Day

The four goal game is a nice drill to help players become aware of open spaces. Four regulation goals are positioned in one half of the field, with a goal at approximately midfield, the two sidelines and on the endline. Younger players may need the goals to be closer together. The group is broken up into two teams defending two adjacent goals with keepers in each. Play begins with a random 50/50 ball as each team scatters to gain possession and attack the open goal. Players should begin identifying when a goal is crowded and seek to find a way to the other goal. Teammates are encouraged to "move off the ball" to create passing angles in this crowded space. An additional ball can also be made live to add a twist to the game.

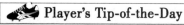

Player's Tip-of-the-Day

Bending your run on defense: When pressuring defenders with the ball as a forward, bend your run towards the goalkeeper to take away the easy back pass and use the sideline as a defender. This forces defenders to dribble out of the back and puts pressure on the ball for a potential turnover.

See a diagram of this drill at beyondsoccer.org.

For more information about today's guest writer, Scott Taylor, log on to beyondsoccer.org.

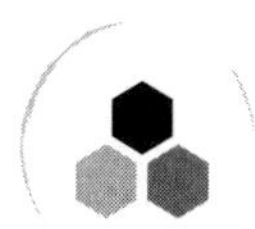

Stretching

1 Chronicles 16:11 (NASB) *Seek the LORD and His strength; seek His face continually.*

Every day in practice, like most soccer teams, we take time at the beginning to do a warm-up and stretch. Stretching is one of those things that you don't necessarily like to do, but a principle that is very important in all sports. Much research has been done to validate the need for adequate stretching before exercise. Studies have proven that there are many benefits that result from proper, consistent stretching over time. As a muscle is stretched, then exercised, that muscle develops a greater range of motion, allowing for more power and a longer stride. Furthermore, stretching helps prevent injury and facilitates healthy muscle growth.

We must invest in the time to stretch our spiritual muscles.

Our Christian walk is very similar. It's easy to go to church each Sunday and stay in our comfort zones, but God calls us to stretch ourselves spiritually. We are called to read His Word, go to Bible studies and attend other Christian events that could enlighten us and deepen our walk with Christ. We are called to step up to Christian leadership positions and invest time in the things that have eternal value. By stretching our minds and growing spiritually we develop the knowledge and spiritual capacity to bring other people to Christ and later teach them what it means to be a Christian.

Stretching before a soccer game or practice is a time-consuming, sometimes boring process that can easily be brushed aside or not taken seriously enough. Similarly, our daily lives are filled with so much that it's hard to invest the time and energy into growing as a Christian. It's easy to sit back and become complacent with where we are, but God calls us to spend time learning about Him, to "*seek His face continually.*" To develop that relationship, we must invest in the time to stretch our spiritual muscles. Pray that God will reveal opportunities around you to learn about Him and make the commitment in your own mind to seek Him more.

Coach's Tip-of-the-Day

After the team completes the group stretching period, always offer to your players five minutes to stretch whatever they need before practice. Every player is different, and some may need to stretch a particular muscle or need an extended warm-up time. Also, be careful to ease into the practice agenda to allow players to continue getting ready. Consider your first drill to be an extension of the warm-up. By giving players an opportunity to take care of their own bodies, you create an environment of accountability and, hopefully, reduce injuries.

Player's Tip-of-the-Day

Make a conscious effort on getting a good stretch before and after practices. Did you know that a good stretch after a hard workout may significantly reduce soreness? Also, during the preworkout time, begin focusing on the practice or game ahead. Think in your mind the things that you want to improve on and visualize your actions in certain scenarios on the field.

Overtime

Hebrews 12: 1-2 *Therefore, since we are surrounded by such a great cloud of witnesses, let us throw off everything that hinders and the sin that so easily entangles, and let us run with perseverance the race marked out for us. Let us fix our eyes on Jesus, the author and perfecter of our faith, who for the joy set before him endured the cross, scorning its shame, and sat down at the right hand of the throne of God.*

I've always liked the saying "Leave it on the field." It is normally uttered by the coach or the captain during the final team gathering before taking the field. It signifies giving it everything you've got, so that when you come off the field, there's physically and mentally nothing left to give; it's the idea of hard work, focus, persistence and maxing out your body for the team. When players work so hard to win a game and then the score is still tied, this saying takes on a new level of meaning. Now you are asked to go out and play overtime while your legs are already barely holding you up. In the case of a golden goal, which means the first team to score wins, it further raises the mental and physical challenges of an already drained team.

Let us fix our eyes on Jesus.

The author of the book of Hebrews wrote, "Let us fix our eyes on Jesus". In our daily routine, that oftentimes feels like the overtime of a game, do we think to focus on Him in our circumstances? So many things crowd our minds. Perhaps we are sitting in our office or driving our car, do we think, 'how can I figure this out' or do we have the faith instead to think, "God, I trust You to figure this out'? I like the word "fix." It doesn't say that we should glance at Jesus; it says we should fix our eyes on him, which means that we should stay steadfast on what He has planned and continue to follow the path He has mapped for our lives. He also promises to be the "*author*" and "*perfecter*" of our faith. Much like an athlete trains to prepare for their sport, God doesn't expect that we suddenly have faith. As the coach, He slowly challenges us and, if we honestly seek Him, He builds within us the endurance we need. During those times in life when it seems like the overtime period will never end, realize that God is your source of strength.

Coach's Tip-of-the-Day

After overtime, many times shoot-outs determine the result of a closely fought battle between two teams. To prepare for this, it is widely believed that practicing penalty shots should be done towards the end of practice or just after wind sprints. To add additional mental pressure, a coach can also choose one player to take the practice penalty kick and explain that if he makes it, the sprints are done for everyone. If he misses, the whole team will do more. Different players should be chosen each time if the penalty kicks are missed in these cases.

Player's Tip-of-the-Day

Pressure training is a drill that can be done with only two or three players. In the case of two players, one tosses the ball in the air, while the other knocks the ball out of the air back to the partner's hands. The object is to challenge the person kicking, by tossing the ball quickly back. Variations can include alternating inside of the foot, laces, thigh-volley, chest-volley and headers. With three players in a group, two hold balls and take turns tossing to the third player. Soft, accurate passes are encouraged to develop your touch on the ball.

Winning in the Second Half

by Richard A. Daughtridge, Pastor/Soccer Coach

It's halftime. The players are huddled around, totally disappointed with the first half. The score is 4 – 0, though not in our favor. "We're making mistake after mistake." The sad eyes that gazed at me, the coach, that day said one thing: Defeat. Everyone on the team was reliving their failures, mentally picturing a slow-motion replay of every mistake. As a coach, I wanted to turn back time, rewind the clock and erase the tapes that they were now playing in their minds. Every coach has been there.

Sound familiar?

Life also offers a mixture of wins and losses, but we must win the most important game, the game of life. The game's prize: eternal life and a personal relationship with God.

I remember my halftime speech that day.

"The first half belongs to the coach. I take full responsibility for the score. Let me take the blame and you focus on what you will do in the second half. The other team is known for its fast speed of play. Let's slow them down! We need to possess the ball more and move the ball up the field. You must win the individual battles. Pass the ball only when you must, and dribble until pressured. Once pressured, I want that player to have options to pass to open players. The first half was mine. This second half belongs to you. Now get out there and win!"

We won that game. I don't think that it was due to those tactics totally, but rather because they were able to erase the failure so that they could see the hope. After the game, one father asked his daughter what the coach said at halftime. She answered, "The coach became guilty for the first half."

As I reflect, it reminds me of the story of how God loved man so much that He erased his guilt and defeat by taking the guilt and punishment on Himself. He died on a cross for you. God offers you an empty slate, forgiveness and a second chance in which He will become your personal coach in all you do. While we were yet sinners, Christ died for us. He accepted the guilt and penalty for all of our wrong, and offers a new playbook for life.

We must all come to a reality that we will have a final whistle in the game of life. How do we make sure we're on that winning team?

If you haven't yet accepted God's forgiveness, take a moment alone and just say this simple prayer:

God. I accept your Son, Jesus Christ, as my Savior. Forgive me for my past and help me to live for You in the future. I give You my life and want to live for You. In Christ's name I pray. Amen.

Now don't stop there. This is only the beginning. He gave us a plan to start us off in the second half. Here are a few kickoff principles and scriptures to begin your second half.

- **Be convinced.** Believe that Jesus Christ is the God Almighty, Creator of the universe, who came in the form of man and accepted the penalty of death on behalf of mankind, offering eternal life to all who believe and accept salvation though Him.

John 3:16-17 "*For God so loved the world that he gave his one and only Son, that whoever believes in him shall not perish but have eternal life. For God did not send his Son into the world to condemn the world, but to save the world through him.*"

- **Be forgiven.** Repent of your wrong. In a single prayer, ask your newfound Savior and friend for His help in becoming the person that He desires for you to become. He will forgive and erase your past.

Mark 1:15 "*The time has come,*" *he said.* "*The kingdom of God is near. Repent and believe the good news!"*

- **Be proclaiming.** Confess to others about your newfound relationship with Jesus Christ.

Romans 10:9-10 *That if you confess with your mouth, "Jesus is Lord," and believe in your heart that God raised him from the dead, you will be saved. For it is with your heart that you believe and are justified, and it is with your mouth that you confess and are saved."*

- **Be baptized.** As commanded in the Bible, be baptized in obedience to His word and to identify with His Church.

Acts 2:38 *"Repent and be baptized, every one of you, in the name of Jesus Christ for the forgiveness of your sins. And you will receive the gift of the Holy Spirit."*

- **Be discipled.** Find a church to attend and be faithful to study, worship and connect with friends in the faith.

Matthew 28:19-20 *"Therefore go and make disciples of all nations, baptizing them in the name of the Father and of the Son and of the Holy Spirit, and teaching them to obey everything I have commanded you. And surely I am with you always, to the very end of the age."*

T-Shirts and Hats

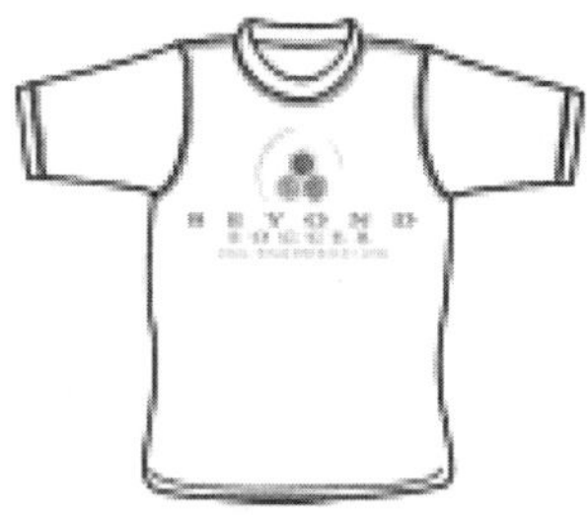

Only $9.95 + shipping

Beyond Soccer T-Shirt

Color: White

Sizes: Medium, Large, X-Large

Type: High-Quality and Durable
100% Cotton Beefy Ts

Order online @ **www.beyondsoccer.org**

Only $11.95 + shipping

Beyond Soccer Hat

Color: Beige

Size: One Size Fits All

Type: Relaxed Fit, Embroidered Logo
100% Cotton w/Adjustable Strap.

Order online @ **www.beyondsoccer.org**

Web Site

We have developed a web site to complement *Beyond Soccer* — the book. By logging onto www.beyondsoccer.org, you can:

- Sign up for our e-mail newsletter for more devotionals, special offers and updates.
- Order Beyond Soccer gear and much more from our online store.
- Send us your questions and comments.
- Find out more about Beyond Soccer Ministries.
- Find links to our partner organizations and friends.
- Read more information about our guest writers and where they are now.
- E-mail us your soccer stories.
- Submit your own devotionals for consideration in future editions.
- Tell a friend about Beyond Soccer.
- Join our mailing list.
- Contact us.